# HYRACOTHERIUM

PREHISTORIC BEASTS

# HYRACOTHERIUM

## MARC ZABLUDOFF

### ILLUSTRATED BY PETER BOLLINGER

**Marshall Cavendish**
Benchmark
New York

Published by Marshall Cavendish Benchmark
An imprint of Marshall Cavendish Corporation

Website: www.marshallcavendish.us

This publication represents the opinions and views of the author based on Marc Zabludoff's personal experience, knowledge, and research. The information in this book serves as a general guide only. The author and publisher have used their best efforts in preparing this book and disclaim liability rising directly and indirectly from the use and application of this book.

Other Marshall Cavendish Offices: Marshall Cavendish International (Asia) Private Limited, 1 New Industrial Road, Singapore 536196 • Marshall Cavendish International (Thailand) Co Ltd. 253 Asoke, 12th Flr, Sukhumvit 21 Road, Klongtoey Nua, Wattana, Bangkok 10110, Thailand • Marshall Cavendish (Malaysia) Sdn Bhd, Times Subang, Lot 46, Subang Hi-Tech Industrial Park, Batu Tiga, 40000 Shah Alam, Selangor Darul Ehsan, Malaysia

Marshall Cavendish is a trademark of Times Publishing Limited

All websites were available and accurate when this book was sent to press.

Library of Congress Cataloging-in-Publication Data

Zabludoff, Marc.
Hyracotherium / by Marc Zabludoff ; illustrated by Peter Bollinger.
p. cm. — (Prehistoric beasts)
Includes bibliographical references and index.
Summary: "Explore Hyracotherium, its physical characteristics, when and where it lived, how it lived, what other animals lived alongside it, and how we know this"—Provided by publisher.
ISBN 978-1-60870-034-9
1. Hyracotherium—Juvenile literature. I. Bollinger, Peter, ill. II. Title.
QE882.U6Z33 2011
599.6—dc22
2009035555

Editor: Christine Florie
Publisher: Michelle Bisson
Art Director: Anahid Hamparian
Series Designer: Alicia Mikles

Photo research by Connie Gardner

The photographs in this book are used by permission and through the courtesy of:
*Minden Pictures:* Mitsuaki Iwago, 10; *Alamy:* vano images GmbH and Co KG, 18

Printed in Malaysia (T)
1 3 5 6 4 2

# CONTENTS

# LITTLE CREATURES

Sheltered by the deep green woods, two small animals nibble eagerly at low-growing clusters of young leaves and fruit. They cannot reach very high—only a couple of feet above the ground—but there is plenty of food, even at this level. Although it is winter, the woods are still warm and humid here, and plants grow quickly. The ground beneath the creatures' feet is very soft, and as they stretch out their necks, they spread their little toes wide to keep their bodies steady.

The animals are a pair, a male and a female. They look something like tiny deer. The male is the larger of the two, but even he is only the size of a fox. Both of them are very nervous, alert for any sound of danger. A slight rustling some distance away makes them freeze immediately. Standing absolutely still, they let the leaf-scattered sunlight flicker over their brown-and-white–striped coats. Now, with their rumps held high

◀ **In the lush, green forests, *Hyracotherium* thrived with the abundance of available food.**

and their heads and shoulders low, they look similar to rabbits about to scamper away in retreat. They hold their pose for a full minute, but they hear no more noises to worry them. Finally they relax and go back to the serious business of eating.

Throughout the quiet surrounding woods are hundreds of creatures just like them. Most of the adults are paired off, and they, too, are now all quietly eating and watching. About three months from now many of the females will give birth. Within a couple of years many of the babies will have babies of their own. For countless generations the process will repeat, and thousands, then hundreds of thousands, and eventually millions of creatures will one day count these shy animals as their ancestors.

None of those many animals will notice, of course, but over the span of 50 million years, big changes will occur. These warm, wet, leafy woods will become the cool, dry, grassy plains of Nebraska in North America. The tiny animals plucking at the leaves will be known by the not-so-tiny name *Hyracotherium*. Most startling of all, the large, majestic descendants of these shy woodland animals will be running over the Nebraska plains, and they will be known as horses.

# AN UNLIKELY HORSE

Children often have much better imaginations than adults. But even the most imaginative child—if she could travel back in time many millions of years—might find it difficult to see a big horse in the future of the little, leaf-eating *Hyracotherium*. Horses are powerful, long-legged creatures, with a large, single-toed hoof on each foot that helps them gallop across open fields and plains. *Hyracotherium*, from its nose to its toes, was not the least bit similar. Yet inside its bones are unmistakable clues telling us that it is the ancestor of today's horse.

*Hyracotherium* was only 10 to 20 inches high at the shoulder and no more than 2 feet long. At its smallest, it weighed only 8 pounds—about the size of a pet cat. Even the very biggest *Hyracotherium* weighed no more than 75 pounds, a weight that puts it in the range of a golden retriever, perhaps, but still nowhere close to a 1,000-pound modern horse.

Nothing about the little animal was big. *Hyracotherium* had a short snout filled with forty-four small teeth suited for chewing soft leaves, buds, stems, and fruit. Holding up its head was a short neck, and holding up its small body were four short legs. The back legs were longer than the front ones, so *Hyracotherium* stood with its hips higher than its shoulders, its back curved in an arch.

On each of its two front feet, *Hyracotherium* had four toes. On each of its rear feet it had three toes. Each one of the toes was covered by a separate little hoof. When walking, *Hyracotherium* held its toes pointing almost straight down. Like a dog, it had thick pads on the bottoms of its feet, behind the toes, to support its weight.

***Hyracotherium* is the ancestor of today's horse. How many differences can you find?**

This image illustrates what *Hyracotherium* looked like when walking. Notice how its foot is pointed straight down.

No one knows for certain what *Hyracotherium*'s coat of fur looked like. Many scientists think that it was probably striped or spotted, like the coats of many small forest-dwelling animals today. The patterning would have helped the small animal blend in with a background of leaves and scattered sunlight and avoid the notice of hungry meat eaters.

# A FAMILY HISTORY

*Hyracotherium* first appeared in North America around 55 million years ago. At this time in Earth's history many new and different kinds of **mammals** were developing. Among them were the ancestors of most mammals we are familiar with today. Some of them, such as mammals with wings— the bats—were highly unusual. But *Hyracotherium* was a member of the much more common collection of mammals that we call the **ungulates**. These are all plant-eating mammals with hooves, and there are two main groups.

**DID YOU KNOW?**

Scientists have different names for different times in Earth's history. The epoch when *Hyracotherium* and many other mammals appeared is called the **Eocene**, which means "the dawn of new time."

One group of ungulates is called the **artiodactyls**, and most of its members are hoofed mammals that have an even number of toes on each foot. They include such animals as cows, pigs, and goats, as well as camels and hippopotamuses. The other group of ungulates, called the **perissodactyls**, is made up of hoofed mammals that generally have an odd number of toes on each foot. This is the group to which little *Hyracotherium* belonged. Its descendants, which include horses, donkeys, and zebras, are perissodactyls as well. So are their other, less obviously related descendents: rhinoceroses and tapirs.

One group of hoofed animal is the artiodactyls. Camels, pigs, and hippopotamuses belong to this group.

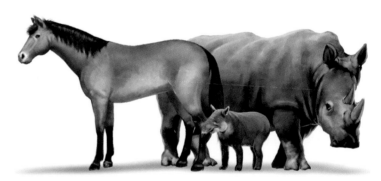

*Hyracotherium* belongs to the group of hoofed animals called perissodactyls. Horses, tapirs, and rhinoceroses belong as well.

# WORDS
# TO KEEP YOU ON
# YOUR TOES

Scientific names can sometimes be confusing. *Artiodactyl* comes from two Greek words that mean "even toed." *Perissodactyl,* meanwhile, means "odd toed." Today, most perissodactyls do in fact have an odd number of toes on each foot, but not all do. Like *Hyracotherium*, a tapir (above), for example, has four toes on two of its feet. What actually determines which group a hoofed mammal belongs to are details of its anklebones and skull. Another difference is in how the animal carries its weight. Perissodactyls, such as rhinos (below left), support most of their weight on their third toe, which is bigger than the other toes. Artiodactyls, such as hippos (below right), place their weight equally on their third and fourth toes.

Scientists knew little about the ancient history of these animals until the middle of the nineteenth century. In the 1870s, however, the North American **fossil** hunter O. C. Marsh found the preserved bones of a small animal that he realized had to be an ancestor of the horse. He gave the animal the lovely name *Eohippus*, meaning "dawn horse." Unfortunately, the British scientist Richard Owen had discovered a similar fossil animal in England thirty years earlier. Thinking that the animal's toes resembled those of a hyrax—a furry African mammal that looks a bit like a very fat guinea pig—Owen named it *Hyracotherium,* or "hyraxlike beast." The name was not nearly as nice as *Eohippus*, but the rules of scientific naming declared that the earlier name was the one the animal kept. To this day, though, many scientists prefer the name *Eohippus*, and they use *Hyracotherium* only grudgingly.

# HYRACOTHERIUM WORLD

The world that *Hyracotherium* knew was quite different from ours. Earth was a lot warmer than it is today. Much of the planet had a climate like Central America's. Average temperatures were around 86 degrees Fahrenheit (30 degrees Celsius). There was no ice anywhere, not even at the north and south poles. Palm trees grew in what is now North Dakota, and fig trees flourished all the way up to Alaska. Green woods and dense, steamy forests blanketed much of the globe. For a leaf eater the world was an endless salad bar.

*Hyracotherium* preferred living not in the crowded forests but in more open woods. There, with its toes spread out to keep it from sinking into the soft, moist ground, it could scurry easily through a maze of feeding spots and hiding places. Also, the woods offered enough open space that a small animal could run quickly if necessary—and sometimes it was very necessary.

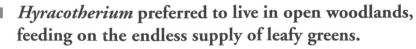
**Hyracotherium preferred to live in open woodlands, feeding on the endless supply of leafy greens.**

During the Eocene many of the large **predators** we know today had not yet appeared. There were no lions or tigers yet, nor any dogs or wolves. But a little leaf eater still had to stay on its toes. Prowling the woods were hyenalike meat eaters called creodonts, which would gladly make a meal of a little horse if they could catch one. Also stalking through the trees were monstrous, 7-foot-tall, meat-eating birds such as *Diatryma*. These feathered giants could not fly, but they had huge, hatchet-shaped beaks, long legs, and powerful feet tipped with deadly claws.

*Diatryma*, **a large flightless, meat-eating bird, may have been a predator of *Hyracotherim*.**

*Hyracotherium*'s only defense against such terrors was its speed. It could dart around bushes and trees more quickly and easily than its toothy or beaky predators. Most of the time *Hyracotherium* was probably able to escape. But not always—fossil discoveries show that sometimes *Hyracotherium* ended up as a predator's dinner.

***Hyracotherium* had the ability to run with great speed and escape from a chasing predator.** ➡

# HOW FAST COULD *HYRACOTHERIUM* RUN?

For an animal its size, *Hyracotherium* was probably pretty quick, able to reach speeds of a little over 30 miles per hour. For comparison, wild horses and zebras can run about 35 to 40 miles per hour.

# LIFESTYLES OF LITTLE HORSES

A typical picture of horses or zebras—the horse's close cousins—will show a herd of animals feeding or running together. Gathering in large groups is normal for grazers, animals that live on open fields or plains and feed on grass. After all, a great number of animals means a lot of eyes on the lookout for predators. It is not normal behavior, though, for browsers—animals that live in the woods and dine mostly on leaves and tender twigs. The woods do not allow room for animals to stick together in herds. As a browser, *Hyracotherium* probably lived as many small forest dwellers live today: in small groups made up of an adult male and a female, along with any youngsters that still need their parents' care. At most, a male may have kept two females with him.

Like many animals the males probably fought each other over those females. The male *Hyracotherium* was larger than the female and had

It is believed that **Hyracotherium** lived in small groups including mother, father, and their young.

longer canine teeth, the pointed teeth at the corners of the mouth. **Paleontologists** assume the bigger bodies and longer teeth were important for fighting off other males.

Male horses today certainly nip at each other with their teeth. Their real weapons, though, are powerful kicks delivered by long, muscular legs and hard, heavy hooves. Those weapons were not available to *Hyracotherium*, whose short legs and little hooves could not have packed much of a wallop, even against another animal its own size. So exactly how one male *Hyracotherium* managed to drive off a rival is still unknown.

# SMALL ANCESTORS, BIG CHILDREN

The modern horse family includes horses, zebras, and the wild asses, or donkeys, of Africa and Asia. All these big, grass-eating mammals are descendants of *Hyracotherium* and many other distinct kinds, or species, of early horses that came after it. Dozens of horse species appeared over tens of millions of years. They all evolved, or changed, to better fit the changing conditions on Earth. The warm, moist Earth of the Eocene became cooler and drier. Forests became sparse woods, and woods became open grasslands. Prowling the woods and grasslands were an army of new predators, among them a variety of big, fast cats and tireless wolves.

Very gradually, horses developed that were able to take advantage of the abundant, tough grass that became available rather than just softer leaves and fruit. Longer legs and bigger bodies gave them more speed.

As the conditions on Earth changed, early species of *Hyracotherium* evolved to meet those changes.

Their feet became better suited for walking on harder ground. Their toes disappeared until only one remained, surrounded by a single hoof, which made the foot perfect for running over open plains. Out in the open they began to gather in large herds for protection.

These changes did not take place quickly, nor all at once, and they did not all happen to all horselike animals. Many horse species kept three separate toes, for example, and for a long time there were many more species

As horses developed with the changing environment, they began to collect in herds on the open plains.

The single remaining toe of the horse is the third, or middle, toe. This is the toe that, millions of years ago, supported most of the tiny *Hyracotherium*'s weight.

of three-toed horses in the world than there were one-toed species. Many horses also remained small, just as many remained browsers rather than grazers.

Today, these different kinds of horses are all extinct. But that does not mean they were in any way less important than the few species that are left. It simply means that the world they were suited for ceased to exist. *Hyracotherium* itself survived on Earth for nearly 20 million years—an impressively long time for a shy little horse.

# TIMELINE

| | |
|---|---|
| 63 million years ago | Earth becomes warmer and wetter. |
| 57 to 55 million years ago | Ancestors of hoofed mammals, both artiodactyls (even-toed) and perissodactyls (odd-toed), appear; *Hyracotherium* appears in North America. |
| 50 million years ago | Global temperature peaks; afterward Earth begins to turn cooler and drier. |
| 30 million years ago | Small, three-toed horses appear. |
| 24 million years ago | Grazing horses evolve in North America. |
| 18 million years ago | Horses become more specialized for eating grass and for running, with larger bodies and longer legs. |
| 15 million years ago | First one-toed horses appear. |
| 4 million years ago | *Equus*, the modern horse, evolves in North America. |
| 2.5 million years ago | *Equus* spreads to Africa and Asia (zebras, asses) and Europe. |
| 10,000 years ago | Ice Age ends; horses become extinct in North America. |
| 500 years ago | European explorers bring horses back to America. |

# GLOSSARY

**artiodactyls** (ahr-tee-uh-DAK-tils)    a group of hoofed mammals that usually have an even number of toes on each foot.

**Eocene** (EE-uh-seen)    a time lasting from about 55 million to 34 million years ago.

**fossil**    the remains of an animal or plant, usually thousands or millions of years old.

*Hyracotherium* (hy-rah-kuh-THEER-ee-uhm)    an ancestor of the modern horse.

**mammal**    an animal that has hair or fur and that feeds its young with milk.

**perissodactyls** (puh-ris-oh-DAK-til)    a group of hoofed mammals that usually have an odd number of toes on each foot.

**paleontologist**    a scientist who studies fossils to learn about the life of the past.

**predator**    an animal that hunts and eats other animals.

**ungulates** (UHN-guh-lits)    the group of mammals that have toes protected by hooves.

28

# FIND OUT MORE

## Books

Clutton-Brock, Juliet. *Horse* (Eyewitness Books Series). New York: DK Publishing, Inc., 2008.

Goldish, Meish. *Fossil Feud: Marsh and Cope's Bone Wars*. New York: Bearport Publishing, 2006.

## Websites

### Fossil Horses

www.flmnh.ufl.edu/fhc/fhc.htm

Fossil Horses in Cyberspace is an excellent kids' site produced by the Florida Museum of Natural History that details the complex evolution of the horse.

### Perissodactyl Mammals

www.zoomdinosaurs.com/painting/Perissodactyls.shtml

This site contains information on some living and extinct odd-toed, hoofed mammals.

# INDEX

Page numbers in **boldface** are illustrations.

# ABOUT THE AUTHOR

Marc Zabludoff, the former editor in chief of *Discover* magazine, has been involved in communicating science to the public for more than two decades. His other work for Marshall Cavendish includes books on spiders, beetles, and monkeys for the AnimalWays series, along with books on insects, reptiles, and the largely unknown and chiefly microscopic organisms known as protoctists. Zabludoff lives in New York City with his wife and daughter.

# ABOUT THE ILLUSTRATOR

Peter Bollinger is an award-winning illustrator whose clients include those in the publishing, advertising, and entertainment industries. Bollinger works in two separate styles, traditional airbrush and digital illustration. He lives in California with his wife, son, and daughter.